Wake Up and Roar

Dear Ron,
Thank you so
much.
Guthema

Also by Guthema Roba

Please Come Home, 2013

Wake Up and Roar

Poetry for Meditation and Awakening

Guthema Roba

NORTH STAR PRESS OF ST. CLOUD, INC.
St. Cloud, Minnesota

ISBN: 978-0-87839-761-7

First edition: June 1, 2014

Printed in the United States of America

Published by
North Star Press of St. Cloud, Inc.
P.O. Box 451
St. Cloud, MN 56302

www.northstarpress.com

Aacknowledgements

Turning these poems into a book wouldn't be possible without a continuous support and love from Astroid, my precious wife, and Homa, my darling daughter—I am truly blessed with you.

I am deeply inspired and moved by the guidance, presence and deep insight from the following friends: Fred LaMotte, Sattva, Helene Averous, Kristy Thompson, Kathryn Graham Wilson, Cezarina Trone, Barbara Jean, O.M. Rohr, Mulumebet Beyene, Shel Brook, Jana Dular, Chinmayi Celina Sochaczewska, Mary McMahons—and many more whose names I have not mentioned here.

I also extend lasting gratitude and love to the staff as well as friends of the Golden Valley library for supporting the flow of this poetry.

I am grateful to Finote Tibeb Literary Center in Minneapolis and *Edge Life Magazine* for publishing my poems in your publications.

To the great staff of North Star Press who published this book—your goodness has always touched my heart.

On the path of spiritual growth and self-inquiry, the following beloved poets, spiritual teachers, mystics and saints have deeply helped me ignite the fire deep in my being that has always been present and also to recognize the same in everyone I come in contact with: My eternal gratitude to Rabindranath Tagore, Krishnamurti, Kahlil Gibran, Herman Hesse, Jalaluddin Rumi, Hafiz, Mirabai, Walt Whitman, Meister Eckhart and many more whose names are not mentioned here.

I bow to everyone who comes to hold this book—you are holding eternity, something that is going to wake up the sun in your own heart. Blessings.

Contents

Mystery to your own mind

Your beauty is a great
mystery to your own mind—
remember your ancient
name before all these
names were given—
when we were still
one and knew each other
very closely.
My heart—
Love more deeply
now.

Force of life

No one I have ever known
or heard of has touched
Happiness through
thinking, intellect,
or sacrifice.
The river of joy
flows right here and
no need of digging
sewer trenches.
The flowing happens
on its own and
the passage is clear.
Be empty as a child—
The force of life
can find you naturally.

The door of your being

Triumphs and achievements
might bring you many medals
and trophies and fame
Nothing is wrong with them.
Only innocence can take you
to the door of your being.
Be wild for love. Be crazy and vanish
into the warmth of the red sea,
Put a book of poetry by your bed.
I assure you, fear will leave your room.
Kindness will return roaring
and you are going to sleep like an infant.
Something will empower
your lips to smile
something will encourage
your eyes to shine.
Your legs will be fearless
and can walk home gracefully.

Roses and moonlights

If
Something inside you
Wants to sing and explode
Into a million galaxies, roses
and moonlights,
Let it happen.
Don't consult it with someone else
Because he-she is going to say
something like this—
Not now, maybe next time
Or something more important
Is on its way . . .

When the mind is still

When
the mind
Is Still
for just a brief instance,
something miraculous
moves through you
And
your entire being
Flowers.

Piece of stone

Courage
Does not mean
To pick up a stone and
Throw it at someone.
It is rather to touch the
Entire universe inside a
Piece of stone.

The one whose eyes are open

The one
Whose eyes are open,
The one
Whose mind is open,
The one
Whose heart is open—
Does not choose to walk
On the road of
Meaninglessness,
On the path
of absolute
Misery.

Knowing your life's purpose

Knowing
Your life's purpose,
Knowing yourself
Makes the world sharper,
Tender-hearted and sweet-mouthed.
This does not just minimize tension.
It ends it completely.

Dissolve into me

If you see yourself
As a prisoner of your
life's circumstances,
Look inside and move
Beyond. Don't hold
anyone responsible.
You hold the key
to the gate of sweetness.
All you need is this reminder.
You've created your own
limitation and anxiety.
You've built a castle that
Could not shelter you because
It is made of fear and bricks.
Don't cling to this madness
Anymore.
Come to the room of
Forgiveness where love
says, Open your arms and
Dissolve into me Now.

On the edge of existence

Don't be afraid
of standing on the edge of
existence—
if you fall,
something wants
to show you what brings
sweetness to honey—
how to break into pieces
and become whole again.

The seed of goodness

You plant
the seed of goodness
When you're able to see
Yourself inside all things.
Then hurting someone else
does not
make you happy
anymore
Because you
hurt yourself.

Be kind

Don't be nervous,
don't be frightened
when I say
the time has come
for you
to return
to yourself.
I just mean—
Be love.
Be here.
Be harmony.
Be kind
So that there is
so much love
we can share.

Infinite splendor

The one
who drinks from
the infinite splendor
of the sea—
from the ocean
of wholeness,
won't complain of
thirst anymore.

Beyond this sky

when you live from your heart,
You break the shell of appearance
and become a connector of
a divided planet, a meeting point
for true companionship—
Beyond this sky there are a thousand skies
blooming in deep silence.

Love me as yourself

Listening
is the most courageous
act of kindness we can give
the world and ourselves.
Inside every single form,
there is a voice
that continues to say—
Love me my friend.
Love me—
love me
as yourself.

Fear makes you blind

The ego's
Ultimate goal is fear
and fear makes you blind
So that you cannot see
your own beauty.
Fear blocks your nose
So that you cannot smell
your own fragrance.
Fear makes you deaf
so that you cannot hear
the music of life.

Your body

Your body listens and
registers whatever
you think and say.
Instead of saying
"I am sick" or "I am tired" or
"I cannot do it . . ."
Why don't you say,
I am celebration
I am the wizard that opens
the doors of laughter,
I am the blend of the sun and
the moon and the sky ....
I am . . .
I am the morning glory,
the pulse of creative energy.
Then you will be it.

Worth kissing

Like a farmer
directing the river to his farm,
direct all your energy and opportunities
towards the kissing of the beloved.
After all
This moment is worth kissing
in the mouth.

It is possible

Making poetry
is building a house
Out of your heart's song.
This is a place of
genuine Intimacy for you
and your beloved alone.
Yes,
Every time I see a tree
warmly cradled within the body
of the earth,
Every time I watch the sun
Pouring herself into the water,
I know it is possible for anyone
not to be afraid of life,
Not to be afraid of light.
I know it is possible for
everyone to be the heart
of the heart of the heart
of the heart—

Flow towards your voice

No matter
how long ago you've left
the house of love—
Please come back.
the door is still open
and you're the only one
who can close it.
Why spend hours
on the mistakes you've made
in the past?
Focus on your wholeness.
Be a spring water and flow
towards your voice.

Direct merging

What you really need now
Is not a broker between you and
the beloved.
Nor time for adjustment.
What you need is a direct love-making,
direct merging and blending
into love itself.

Because you are enough

The world is very demanding and harsh at times
and there are people who count the number
of years they lived
and worry so much because they think
they've achieved nothing worthwhile.
My friend,
life does not demand anything from you.
That fact that you're here is enough.
Because you're enough.

Speak of light

Speak of light
With no fear
Because light is not scary.
Light is who you are.
The one who is afraid of light
Is afraid of himself.
Speak of beauty
my friend.
Speak of the one
who steals
your words and curves them
Into songs.
sing of the one
who breaks into your bedroom
and wakes you up from your
nightmare.

What comes from the origin

You are
not running for office.
Stay very close to the truth.
What comes from the origin
Is original.
Spill what is in the heart's cup.
Abandon the defense mechanism
You've learned. Love does not
defend herself. Nothing can break her.
Don't listen to fear.
It drives you to a place where people stand
In line to buy guns.
Look at your eyes,
you're a power-house
of forgiveness.

Sense of deficiency

The ego pushes you
either to be against or
In favor of because
It has no courage to stand
In the center on its own.
Out of deficiency and fear
It either wants you to follow
or to be followed
and it does not know
there is a region inside you
where you can be
truly yourself.

Acute hunger

Everywhere we look
someone is busy explaining things
to someone else.
So much words and labor go
into the conversation.
There is no space left in between.
It seems there is an acute hunger
Just to say something.
What is true
does not require clarification
because it is simple and
direct and original
most of all the heart knows
it already.

Beyond the form

Don't pay so much attention
to the forms you see,
including your own form.
attempting to find happiness
through the cosmopolitan magazine
Separates you from aliveness.
Forms are not real because
they keep changing and changing and
What you see today won't be the same
ten years from now.
If you want stability,
See beyond the form and
recognize the one
that is Changeless.

How much caffeine

How much caffeine,
How many alarm-clocks
does a person need
to wake up?
Does a moonless sky say
He is abandoned?
Is he afraid of being alone?
Humans complain about nature
All the time.
They criticize and blame her
for everything.
Does criticism bother her?
This is not a question at all
Nor a test nor inspection.
It is a sound of a seed
breaking the ground to
smell the sun.
Drink it now
Don't postpone
ecstasy.
Don't save joy
in your bank
account.
Drink it now.
All of it because
there is no shortage.

Zero interest rate

Giving
is your nature.
give yourself
from the place of
zero interest rate
And no profit.
You're showing the world
The meaning of abundance where
The giver and the receiver neither lose
Nor gain but radiate like a white full moon.

There are days

There are
days when your energy overflows
And you want to kiss everyone you meet
In the street.
At other times, you can hardly
Get out of your bed for breakfast.
Some days , you get out in the crowd
And show off your looks.
Other times, you bury your head
In the desert and snore—
Some days you give off sweet colors.
Other times, you settle for black
And white—
Leave all this struggle behind.
Start life not from where you've left
But from nothing
Look how the wild animals
Snuggle with the forest.
Begin love affair with the one
who can turn your arms
Into wings of living flames.
The one who can transform your lips
Into fresh bay leaves;
your eyes into ever-burning lamps
And your heart into a brilliant sun.

All that is nourishing

All that is nourishing,
All that is kind,
All that makes us
Sing and dance
arises from inside,
From the heart.
That is more ancient,
much closer
To you than your beliefs.

The one who has forgiven

The one
who holds
The altar of kindness inside himself
The one who has forgiven—
Is free
And does not store fear or guilt anymore
because kindness removes
All that is not true.
Love erodes all that is
not you.

More closeness

I want to start friendship
with you—
Life said to me.
I spread myself under her feet
and became a garden.
She became a rose and
Released sweet aroma.
She said,
I want more closeness.
I turned myself into a flute.
She picked me up from the floor
And kissed me—
I started singing fearlessly.

Promise me today

Promise me today,
dear friend that,
you are not going to
wait your entire life
for someone
to make you happy—
Look how beautiful you are!
The entire autumn sky
wants to seek shelter
Inside your being.

Tender house

Be loving and most compassionate
in your movements and words
and thoughts—
We're all being held inside
This tender house called
the heart.

Here is not a place

Here
Is not a place.
It is grace
pouring into
grace.
It is
the state of
Wholeness.
look at the sky
and the falling leaves
and the wind moving
the trees—
that is HERE.
Feel how your feet
take turns to kiss
the earth.
That is here too.
everything is here.
you are the only one
who is away.

What does a rose need to bloom?

What does a rose
need to bloom?
What makes the ocean
fragrant?
What brings eloquence
to our lips?
Ever since love took-over,
my entire body has become
a divine lamp and the heart
grew deeper—
What is there
I cannot hold
today?
What is there
I cannot embrace?

Making a living

Don't settle with making a living
or paying bills.
Be the art of living and
the mystery of life itself.
Stay present when you
tie your shoes
or brush your teeth . . .
or when you drive—
your heart's light
Can set the sky
On fire.

Who is sitting closer to you

Who
Is sitting closer to you
than your own mouth?
who is putting your songs
In the lips of a nightingale?
don't judge a horse by its teeth.
look the way he touches the
ground with his hooves
and his wild presence flying
into the sky through his
mane.

Our being here

Our being here
Is a rain falling from the sky of
Splendor into a warm heart of the earth.
It needs nothing other than
Its own fullness.
here, each drop curves
Itself into poetry
and every glass of wine overflows
with endless joy.
let the autumn leaves
and the wind wrestle
until they fall down together
and vanish into bliss,
into the dust of longing.
let this innocent lovemaking
repeat itself a hundred times
a day!

The horse

A man sits on the horse
and beats it with harshness.
He did not know the horse was
rushing towards his longing.
Be grateful to your old boat
that wants to sink—
the ocean is there waiting
to take care of you.

Running away

Last evening
I was going for a short walk—
In our neighborhood,
Those Long, elegant trees were rising
To touch the half dark sweet moon.
Birds were singing of aliveness.
In the highway
People were speeding—
They were running away
from what expands them,
what makes their hearts sing.

Glow

Glow
because you are
here for that.
the earth responds
to your fragrance
with sweet dance.
don't be afraid
of doing anything that
wakes you up in the mornings
and makes you erupt into
a thousand flowers
Even if this means
Annoying your sleepy neighbors.

Come closer to me

You've learned
A tremendous amount
of worries ever since you were born.
come closer to me, dear one,
until you can see with your own eyes
the full face of innocence.
Don't compare—
Stop flirting with
what does not sparkle.
make peace with love.
Separation from your own sweetness
is the toughest choice
you can ever make.

Like innocence

Ever since I saw you, you're a big boy.
Have you ever been a child, daddy?
my daughter said to me one morning—
Yes, I said
I've always been a child,
A very grown up child—
I did not find a word to explain further—
we both became the ocean of silence.
be straight like innocence,
like the face of clear sky that
cannot hide its ecstasy
and walk with grace
on the ground
of eternity.

Endless splendor

Life
has appointed you to speak.
So speak of goodness.
of an endless splendor
of the heart seething with holy fire.
today you're going to rise beyond
the hemispheres of opposites—
heaven and hell, good and evil,
Right and wrong—
So that you can enter here
And sit with the beloved.
And everyone you meet
In the desert of need
be a sweet mist or spring water.
thousands of dry throats
will burst into glorious songs
again—

No substitute

Your feelings and emotions—
your endless thoughts—
your constant effort to exceed
or to meet the world's
expectation or
just to survive—
all of these do not matter.
The universe knows you
As a precious gift for which
there is no substitute.

An opportunity

If an ordeal
chooses to come your way
what does that mean to you?
Your are being refined.
An opportunity arises
One more time because it
Is time for you to wake up and
dance with total acceptance.
The journey completes itself
Where it precisely started.
You are united with the
Beloved.

Grapes into sweet raisins

Don't tell yourself
abundance is beyond your territory.
In your eyes dwell, sparkling seas
and roaring oceans.
only when you forget what you are,
you begin feeling like an abandoned
castle.
Respond to all life's messages
with deep love and gratitude.
Don't be a moist wood
that gives off smoke.
Be a distilled wine and a polished
mirror—
In the society that keeps looking for
something that has never been missing,
your presence can turn
grapes into sweet raisins.

Come

Come
to the meeting of lovers
not the way loneliness
drives you
nor from the place
that seeks acceptance—
Come to this gathering
because you are
plenty and you've so much
to share.

Like Bird

Once you find the courage
and willingness to know love,
Something hits your inside
and you will stop preaching about it.
you will stop thinking about it.
you will stop planning about it.
you will Listen and when you listen,
you won't be afraid to sit with yourself in
deep silence. you won't be afraid to laugh.
when you listen, you will blossom and
your beauty erupts all over, healing
every single crack of the world.
when you listen, you are yourself again
and you will find the power to sing like a bird
on a tree branch.

Be fresh air

Stop resistance. Be fresh air and
Sail beyond cause and effect. You're
happiness.
don't host misery in your
Guestroom. Life wants
to shine through you.

Walking on the red carpet

When all is said and done
the mind and body will be tired of living in the past
and telling old stories . . .
walking on naked earth makes more sense than
walking on the red carpet—
That means
there is a greater chance for you
to return to a place
of sanity where you can
merge with life.

With all your breath,
Be humble.
With all your being,
love.
let whatever you do
dance with grace.
Inside of you,
There is something
that is
Unnamable,
Inerasable,
Unbreakable
Unrepeatable
It radiates beyond the
Sun and the moon.

The only path available

The moment
you start to believe that
your path is the only
path available,
you' are contributing to the
rising of the turbulent
world.

The direction

The direction
they have given you
can only take you where
the road ends.
If you want
to go beyond,
You need to find
your own.

Wild flower

What is there
we need to research and understand
about Each other?
Who has ever felt
the breath of God
with laboratory equipment?
something we don't see
continues to turn rocks
and sands
and humans into brilliance.
the ego pays
attention only to our differences
but from inside
everyone is a wild flower.

The very instance
love touches you,
it makes you more humble, soft and tender
opening you further and deeper
so that you can contain more
love and tenderness
until you become the sea.

Bridges

We are here to build
Bridges not prisons
to be the mother of the ocean—
and dispense liquid love
In the city of thirst—
to mirror on our face not misery
but the coral reef of harmony.
to touch the cord of this immense
Beauty and let the world
spin with love.

River of wine

Nothing is short.
wake up and listen
to the drum of grace playing
everywhere. inward and outward.
In your garden, the river of wine flows —
you are standing between the
two bridges connecting a thousand wild hearts.
be willing to relinquish whatever
does not serve your purpose.
cooperate with everything
that helps you look into
your own depth.
Most of all, relax,
Relax my dear friend.
The hands that guide the cosmos
are knocking on your door.

Dissolve more—

This freshness
This sweet jesus-buddha inside—
That opens and expands us
That makes the sun
Circle around us—
what is awake
even when the body is asleep—
talk less, my friend. speak less
sing more. listen more. burn more and
dissolve more—
the same drum is playing
everywhere.

Your hermitage

When your sky crumbles on your head
and the ground beneath you
Cracks open and can no longer
support you—
When your house burns down
and the locust wipes out your crops—
When almost everything around you
Seems to be falling into dust
and there is nothing to hold—
let the voice in the center of your
being be your song—
and let your heart be
your hermitage.

Wake up and roar

There is something
you are born with.
That is a true gift.
gaze inside—
clean yourself from
what is not organic.
Don't be content with
a candle light.
you've the ability to turn
your dreams into fireworks
and ten thousand sparks.
Now, this endless snoring in your
sleep is enough—
let your beauty wake up and roar.
Let a bird grow
more wings than feathers.
She knows when and how to leave
her cage and fly
into mystery of existence

A simple act of kindness

A simple act of kindness
You bring to what you do,
Such as being yourself,
or going to
sleep when your body
is tired—
Deepens the dimension
of the heart.

The way I love you

The way
I love you is like this—
I will keep singing and singing for you
Until my throat aches—
Until my voice fades—
until you wake up and see with your own eyes
everything and everyone is incomprehensibly
divine.

Go anywhere, do anything.
Life is not challenge-free
Until you accept the challenge
as your dear companion with whom you
Want to snuggle and laugh and share
poetry of the inner harmony.

Divine dance

Without resisting,
when you are ready
to vibrate and pulsate
with the frequency of life—
That is the most divine dance.

Absolute tyranny

The compulsive need
To be right all the time
Is an indication of a very
strong egoic mind pattern.
Unless it is observed very closely
and consciously,
it can turn itself into
an absolute tyranny.

Original seed

Despite this commotion
and deep darkness
the world is moving
through each day,
everyone we see around us
is the reminder of light
and this clear seeing
is the return to the
original seed.

A single sip from your joy

Don't tell me this, dear one.
Deep truth cannot be told. It only can be
experienced.
A thousand dawns and sunrises keep
gravitating to your eyes.
I know what that means—
A single sip from your joy
can intoxicate the entire
world hungry for love.

Free from memories

When you struggle—
When you really struggle—
You cannot be here with me
At this moment
Because you probably
take yourself Seriously.
Or you just forgot who you are.
If you stop and look for a moment
If you look with clear eyes free
From memories, free from stories,
You can see the sun
Wanting to turn herself
Into you.

Sometimes

Sometimes
the ocean roars in the desert.
sometimes the moon rises in the day
and the sun at night.
This is because the roaring
and the rising is from inside.

In the world

In the world
that is always looking, looking, looking
and cannot see,
where shouting is venerated than listening;
The world that has long forgotten how to smile.
I feel immensely grateful because
I am still moved beyond description
by the beauty that wants to burst
and makes itself fully available.

When we gather for a dance

When we gather for a dance
in the guest house of life
we're no longer guests and
no introduction is needed
because life knows herself
with sharp precision.

Where poetry can grow

Just like singing or kissing,
laughter has the ability to diminish conflict,
reduce pain and create a lush space
inside us where poetry can grow and flourish.

The real wild one

I came to your door
dear friend, to wake you up
from the memory of your past love-making
Because when you wake up
you will make love to the real wild one.

Stay close to your smile.

Stay close to your smile.
Because the ocean felt your beauty so deeply,
She wanted to rise and kiss tender eyes of the sky.
Stay close to your smile.

Meeting obligations

Forget meeting obligations.
You are here to focus on
who you are right now.
Keep knocking on the door of love
Until it wakes up and engulfs
all of your being, until you become fluid
like rain, soaking all
things.

Open the door

The one
Who awakens the skies,
The one
Who moves the winds,
The one
Who lights up our face
Is here.
Please open the door.

The flute

The flute
in your hand, my friend
plays with such grace
and passion.
Because you've given it
your whole self.
You've given it your heart
and your music.

Forgiveness

It does not matter
How you look.
People are going to judge you
When you go out to the world.
It is not people who judge you—
It is the conditioned mind.
It is fearful thought.
This opens the opportunity
For you to extend forgiveness and love,
To send understanding and light
For the ignorance directed towards you.

A thousand dark caves

Gaze inside.
speak from the place
of no fear,
from pure emptiness
where wings remember
the purpose of flying,
your words will turn to
milky ways and shine
A thousand dark caves.

Vanish into sunlight

In this life time,
I've known
a thousand positions of
lovemaking—
one of which
is to leave
your name behind
and vanish
into sunlight.

There is only this love

There is
Nothing in this moment—
no left or right. no buyer or seller.
no television and no news.
nothing comes and nothing goes—
no fame or conflict—
there is only this love
there is only this silent song
of the beloved, of the heart—
Child of innocence
If you can only stop worrying
and look inside, you can find me—
If you can only stop thinking
and listen,
you can hear me.

All-consuming sweet fire

You've been taught for years
that you will meet God
not now but when you die—
my dear companion,
I don't want you to wait any longer.
please throw away your patience
and lose your dignity
And run fast towards this
all-consuming sweet fire.

Sacred bread

How many times a day
have you doubted your inner light?
a single step that is taken without
doubt can bring you to the doorway
of a bosom friend called Joy.
if you want to bake a sacred bread,
close those cookbooks on your shelf
and open your heart.
you can find all ingredient
inside here.

Original simplicity

A beautiful gift ever to
give someone
is your true essence—
your original simplicity
your emptiness—
not your worries or fear.
The world around you
Is already dense with
false identity.

Flow

Everything
Is in such a ceaseless flow.
The passage of seasons—
Meeting and parting of paths—
Demolishing of the old
And emerging of the new—
If you cannot find something/someone
where you've left it,
Don't be disappointed.
The universe is dancing, dancing, whirling and
spinning
and refining Itself.

Luminous beings

When we meet
as luminous beings
not as persons with
problems and stories,
we're meeting at the
very matrix of life
and there is
no room for human drama.
a moist clay will
turn itself into a jar because
it wants to contain this glory.

When you change

When you change,
everything around you changes.
When you start an intense love affair
with life,
your beauty awakens thousands from sleep
because you are igniting a holy fire
and touching the root of the universe.

Earthdance

Don't try to be nice.
Just be who you are.
someone will
find faults with you anyway.
Your responsibility is not
to react or defend yourself.
it is to love and accept
yourself fully,
when this happens,
You've touched the deepest
core of earthdance
and the rain of grace pours
on you from inside-out
washing away all your
doubts.

The beginning of time.

May you find the courage
today, to look at the sun
and know her
as your own heart!
that alone is enough
to clear all confusion
gathered since the beginning
of time.

Between right and wrong

When your choice
Is to be here with what is,
Life jumps, startled by her
own beauty and you will
no longer struggle between
right and wrong or good and evil—
and every single particle in your body
weaves a brilliant light.

Pointing to the sky

You
are pointing to the sky
from a distance
as if the sky is not you.
move a little closer
and touch his kindness.
Don't you find it exhausting to be
a stranger to what makes
you bloom?
For years
my ancestors have danced
around the fire.
It is now time
to jump inside
and burn.

You are not divided anymore

A friend comes unannounced,
rips you wide open,
takes out your garbage and fills
you with light—
isn't that a true love?
now you are not in pain any more.
You are not divided anymore.
You are not fearful anymore.
You are a fragrant song playing
in the heart of all Beings.

Beyond wanting

How close are you today
To your heartbeat?
Do you hear the music of the sun?
What did the fresh snow whisper
To your warm feet this morning?
The mind thinks you have a ring
Of remembrance on your finger—
The truth is
You are the ring of radiance
Around the galaxies.
You are the molecules and the dust
From which the moon is made.
A friend is the one who wakes up
and finds You inside her laughter.
Don't run away.
Meet everything as they
Come your way—
Pain, pleasure, fear, sorrow—
But don't cling to anything
And anyone.
The one who has arrived
Is beyond wanting.

This endless road

Oh child of daybreak!
Your travels
on this endless road
will leave you extremely
discontent and fatigued
until you find yourself dancing
inside the circle of light
drawn by the hands of innocence—
then there won't be any part
inside you that cannot smell
the warmth of this love.

Hands of now

Don't argue with what is true.
Pursue nothing outside of you.
See with the eyes of now
Touch with the hands of now.
You are touching the one
That touches every being.

A wedding ritual

Once
I went to a wedding ritual
where form was being married
to formless—
The intense aroma and the courage
of this pouring love stayed with me
forever.
Dear friend,
Life becomes the eternal dance
For the one who can walk
With one foot on the ground
And with the other deep in the
Heart .

When two egos meet

When two egos meet
they start friction and
Conflict because the
meeting is happening
From the place of great
deficiency, a zone that
Constantly bemoans to be
filled with something
other than its forgotten
Song—
When hearts meet,
It becomes communion
And celebration—
The world dies into it.
It is the meeting of the beloveds
disguised as persons.

Learning rules

A child
who grows up busy
learning rules, protocols,
guidelines and standards—
cannot get the chance
to be himself/herself
nor can she/he have the room inside
for the one that really
matters most.

Who is making the bed?

Who's making the bed
and putting out candles . . . ?
I don't know about you.
I've become a drunkard
and died into the
light of creative force.
time and distance does not
exist for me and I have not
yet done making love
to the moon.

Restore rain to the desert

Without naming
Or defining the essence,
When you see things
The way they are,
You restore rain
To the desert—
You free yourself and
the world From deep pain.

Polish the gold

Living in the monasteries
For a thousand years
and meditating every day
Does not guarantee you
Freedom from suffering.
The question is
How willing and courageous
are you to move inside
and polish the gold
within you?

Ten thousand illusions

If this journey
does not take you
to a region where
we are all one,
then it is only a dream
and you need to wake
up now.
ten thousand illusions
are not worth half a glimpse
into a heart drenched
in love.

Your business

Anything can happen
and yet nothing can destroy
what is already here.
don't judge or control
or accuse what wants to emerge
in this very instance.
that is not your business.
your business is to
jump into its depth
and kiss all of it.
all of it from bottom
to the top and inside.
then something rips you wide
open and your heart flowers.
Your silence becomes the
the bed of roses
And your words become
butterflies.

Dissolving hug

Last evening,
I almost stepped on
An empty, cold cocoon
Left by a butterfly
and paid deep homage.
It tells delicious stories
Of liberation.
Celebrate my friend,
Celebrate.
Any flowing towards yourself
Is homecoming.
Forgive anything that
makes you forget
You're breathing—
Anyone that stands between you
And the light in your eyes
Badly wants your dissolving hugs—

Knowing is not partial.

Knowing is not partial.
It is total. It is whole
it is not something you acquire
it is already there. It is the smile in every eye
we see, the aroma in every food that is being cooked,
the love in every ground we touch.
Knowing yourself also
means knowing all beings because
in your chest there is a song all
mouths sing. Inside of you there is light
pouring into all seeing.
As this poem moves through, I feel the sky bowing to
the ocean inside of me.

Your Dream

Everyone has a dream but
having a dream is not enough.
Let the sun shine and erupt
on your dream.
Let your dream wake up
and sing.

You are the one

The one who loves you
Takes away your old shoes
and gives you wings
so that you can rise and touch
the sky in your heart.
She bakes bread from sunlight
and feeds your longing.
Then you know
you are the one you've been longing for.
You are the one you've been waiting for.

Drinking from the spring

Most radiant being—
My friendship with you
Is not hierarchical. It is not based on
any belief systems, gender or religion
One cannot understand it with the mind.
It has no expiry date because time cannot enter here.
It is called seeing-looking with one heart;
drinking from the spring that never dries.

Hallway to a Visitor

Whatever feelings or waves of emotions
you suppress or resist,
be it joy or anger or sexual urge—
It nags you constantly;
and wrecks your foundation;
and shakes your roots;
and steals you from life's eternal songs.
For whatever wants to show itself through you
For whatever wants to appear on your door
Be a doorway,
Be a window facing the sun.
Be a hallway to a visitor.

Cycle of Fear

Whenever we meet someone
from the field of now
it is no longer someone.
we are meeting with ourselves.
We just entered the heart
and found a soulmate awaiting.
In the face of this knowingness;
In the eyes of this beauty;
The cycle of fear and competition
Dissolves immediately.

Your Giving

You feed the homeless
Or give donation or charity.
Then you tell the mind what you've just done.
Then the mind wants something in return, you know,
such as publicity or credit or fame
Or even if possible to erect
a statue in your name.
My friend—
Let your giving be unheard music your heart sings.
Not to build credits nor to make news
Let your giving be like the evening breeze
that leaves no trails or like a morning sun
Shining on a green meadow on the hill without a
sound.

What Opens Our Eyes

Reason is not complete on its own.
What opens our eyes in the early mornings
And fills them with sweet light;
why doors open before we even touch them;
Then again, we stand on a bridge between light and
shadow and do not know which one to choose from.
Love emerges out of nowhere and says:
I know where you want to go.
come.

Presence

From the sun
I learn how to radiate light—
From the sky
How to rise beyond time and space
How to be infinitely vast and limitless.
From the earth
How to be abundant and loving
and passionate.
From the ocean
The wisdom of pure presence
and deep Listening
to myself.

The Moment You Touch Me

The heart
Is swung wide open
And how it has grown so much, I cannot tell.
And I am no longer satisfied with facts and figures.
That is why, beloved one,
The moment you touch me,
I melt.

Ultimate clarity

Once
The awareness of who you are sweeps you by
surprise,
Nothing in this world really matters much
and no one will make you feel miserable nor happy
because
The inner workings of the cosmos will find you
With the ultimate clarity.

You're home now

You may know sometimes
and sometimes you may not.
But you're on your way and with each step you take
you make poems within poems. you are peeling
layers after layers
because you know the deeper you move the more
intense it becomes.
So you keep moving. On your way a snake stops you.
he blocks your way.
You look at him and smile with all your eyes and
face. the snake suddenly loses his venom and says to
you: May the light inside you guide your way!
May music follow you wherever you want to go! You
keep going. You cross the sea of thought.
You cross the field of fear and worries.
You look around with new eyes.
Then you want to sit there and rest a little bit.
Something very beautiful overtakes you
and you want to scream with joy. Oh Goodness! It
feels so damn good here!
even before you stretch your hands you touch the
face of God.
You feel her-his gentle hands in yours. You ask her-
him "Why is it so good to be here?
she-he looks at you with tender sweet eyes and would
say:- here is where you began your journey. You are
home now.

Child in the Neighborhood

As soon as
the child is in the neighborhood . . .
as soon as the teacher is in town . . .
as soon as the beloved is in the city . . .
We know it.
we know it immediately
Because something inside us splits wide open.
The heart inside us expands.
the bird inside us begins to sing
the wizard inside us comes alive
the flame inside us begins to burn.
The moon inside us awakens.
As soon as the child is in the neighborhood
we become that child and that child becomes
us.

Underneath all forms

One day
a shepherd confronts a starving tiger
who wanted to eat one of his precious sheep.
Instead of fighting with him, the shepherd sat
on the hill and played him a flute.
The tiger forgot his hunger, sat down
and listened with love pouring from his eyes.
wherever you are,
whatever you do, there is nothing
in this planet that is not you.
underneath all forms you see,
there is you.
beneath all sounds you here
there is you
beneath all dances
there is you.

Let There Be Light

Let there be light.
Let the light be you.
Let there be love.
Let the love be you.
Let there be peace.
Let the peace be you.

What Happens?

Last night
a poem tapped on my ribs
from inside and I woke up
to the sound of a heavy rain—
it rained all day today, too
and the ground opened her
pores to receive these
deep blessings.
What happens
when we love
without conclusion,
without doubt,
without expectations?
What happens
when we drop
our desire to be perfect
and dissolve into the
depth of who we are?
What happens?

Love Room

Don't come into the love room
with decisions already made,
with preloaded software and
lists of expectations.
It is not your knowledge,
It is not your accomplishments
it is not your fame
that love wants.
It is rather your pure heart.
It is your authenticity
that love wants from you.

With the Love Like This

With the love like this
churning me,
with the love like this rocking me,
How can I be afraid?
How can I hide in the dark corners
and moan?
the one who can intoxicate me
is here.
the one who can turn me on
is here.
how can I hide in the dark corners
and moan?
With the love like this
trees want to tear off their bark
and dance in the streets.
everyone and everything
want to turn into spirit
and soar the skies.

Two Hands

Two hands come together
to wash pain
from each other.
this is the meeting of two petals
on the same plant.
they emit fragrance,
they make love like two rivers meeting.
if you are not fully here in this meeting of hands,
you cannot make love—
you make frictions.

If a Friend Goes Missing

What is it in you,
radiant one,
That opens me easily
As soon as I hear you?
What is it in you
that makes me want
to sit by you and sing?
Some days reason says
you are not here, left
not to return anymore.
Days and nights go by
without hearing from you.
I move deeper one more time
Beyond the stories of
birth and death,
beyond coming and leaving
beyond my world and your world.
Then here you are, my friend
never left, never missing.
Here you are, beloved.
Since then I tell everyone I know:
If a friend goes missing
don't call the police,
nor toss a rosary.
nor consult the oracles
go inside of you, instead.
Go inside of you.
She is there.

You are not your credit history

When you know
You are not your life's circumstance,
When you know
You are not your credit history,
When you know
You are not your political issues?
Then your sorrow radiates
like the face of the full, white moon
in the night sky.

In the Lap of Your Heart

Cuddle yourself
warmly, intimately and deeply in the lap of your heart
then
even homelessness cannot
deprive you from your true home.
prison cells cannot keep you
a prisoner.

The Nile

When the time is right
The Nile himself will stop wandering
in the desert carrying mud and silt.
When the time is right
the Nile will stop dreaming
and pump his last drop
into the ocean.
Now we all have grown up
and it is time to stop talking.
Let the beautiful one speak through us.
Let him settle in, rise and then
start a revolution inside us.
Let him build the fire
that burns fear and worry.

A Space Where the Healing Happens

Sometimes a person who's very close to your heart
might say something unkind to you. What comes to the
mind immediately is to react using more unkind words.
This is called defense. That is the way of the egoic
mind. Defense. Who are you defending yourself from?
Who are you fighting? Have you seen the earth
defending herself from earthquake? Have you ever seen
someone who fought cancer and won . . . ? Have you?
It is important to watch where these feelings are arising
from. The person, who is saying harsh words to you, is
the part of you that needs healing. It is your own
shadow hungry for some light, craving for a clean glass
of water. Can you be the light for him? Can be a space
where the healing happens quickly?

Like an Arrow

Like an arrow
Flung with great precision and focus
Your radiance struck me hard
And found my center.
And all logical arguments and reasoning
Start falling off my hand
Crushing on the ground.
When you are dazzled
By the beauty of this moment
You won't ask or don't even care
To know what is coming next.

You Barter Your Gold

You've been doing
a lot of forgetting, my friend.
You look for a broken glass
under the garden of roses.
You barter your gold with another gold
because the mind tricks you into believing
that your gold is less shiny than that of your neighbor.
The one who brings clarity to your eyes,
the one who sends sweetness to your lips
and the one who perfumes your breath with fire
is kissing your forehead
to wake you up from your dreams.

We Kept Coming Closer

Every being was moving but it was
Towards itself
We were not just dancing
we became the dance itself
We were not just singing. We became the song itself.
All the words have left our mouth.
We were drunk and yet we still know
Where the home is.
Our feet touched something and came to a complete stop.
It was the supreme crochet in the center,
holding all things together.
and we could not walk away from here.
How can we walk away from here?
We kept coming closer
and closer and closer.

You Are Not Alone

A flame caught me this morning
and I fell down on a tulip's bulb
who said to me:
Look! you are not alone;
I am on flame too.
Do you think this meeting
is accidental?

Owner's manual

The ocean
Is more than enough for all of us.
Why do you prefer to live in the puddle?
Oftentimes, you spend so much energy to be
Who you are not
Truth to tell, who you are does not demand anything.
It does not need a driver's license nor the owner's manual.
Be simple, organic and undiluted.
Be inflammably, insanely alive.
You will see if the ego does not
Crumble and melt by your
Inner knowing.

Your to-do list

You plan so much.
you set goals after goals after goals and
Your table staggers with your to-do list
and you think you're running behind.
Now
Forge your friendship with this moment
And ask your heart
to show what is real
Then the mind turns into
A brilliant, humble servant
Not a tyrannical master any more.

Time for a Walk

Evening has come
and sweet-mouthed one
has returned to the village.
Stars are out again. The sky, standing fearlessly naked,
paints himself with love.
What else does he know other than love?
Underneath, flew the birds following the song
They heard last night before they went to sleep.
Life is so beautiful my friend. Life is delicious.
My feet want to kiss the ground this evening.
It is time for me to go for a walk.

Wide open

I know not
what happened exactly
but as soon as
I felt your presence
Something from inside
That seemed to be
under a thousand locks
Cracked open and whispered;
Listen! Don't tell anyone
you saw me. I can be contagious.
I can spread like forest fire
and drive millions wild with love.
As soon as
I smelled you in the distance,
The seas started rising and rising until
they flooded the houses
built on worries and grief;
and the winds carried your scent
and went horse racing.

Heart of the Porridge

Is your sobriety and decency
serving the purpose you are here?
Is it pointing to the song that is hidden from you?
It is not enough to be a wine expert.
Be drunk and merge with the wine itself
Then spill kindly and pour into yourself.
Drop the last layers of your garment
And look how beautiful you are.
For love's sake, don't save this drunkenness for tomorrow.
Hold the spoon firmly and delve it into the heart
Of the porridge.

Name of the Sky

You said
You did not want to know
the name of
that sky.
You said
You did not want to know
the name of
those stars.
You said
You did not want to know
the name of
This tree.
This tells me something very profound, dear one.
Through you,
The earth's beauty is finding her center within us.
Through you
This being human is flowering
And soaring above nametags and
mentally constructed labels.

Beehive

I am a beehive in the wilderness
You're a dark honey
occupying my heart.
A brief remembrance of you
sweetens my whole being and turns
me into a fragrant forest.
Then I start forgetting small details
such as my grocery list or wearing my watch
or marking my calendar.
Is it possible to be confined in a cage
and count nickels and dimes
when being in your presence just for a moment
transcends everything?

I Want Intoxication!

I want intoxication!
I said to the sun this morning.
Who wants intoxication?
She wanted to know.
The wild mule inside of me
wants intoxication, I said.
I am glad you asked, she said.
She opened up fully and
asked me to enter.
I did as she said.
I don't remember for how long I was inside.
Does time exist when you're inside love?
Now that I have learned,
all the urge of kicking and restlessness,
all the sign of resignation,
all that I knew and treasured
is transformed into being.

A harp

I am a harp
wildly on fire by the touch
of your beautiful hand.
Please, come play
me again and again and again.

Someone Saying to a Flower

I heard someone saying to a flower:
Don't you feel lonely here by the abandoned bridge,
just yourself and no one else? Aren't you scared?
The flower replied with a smile:
Listen my friend:
In the morning a gentle, cool breeze caresses me with the
kindest hand
I have ever felt on me.
During the day, the sun blows my breath away with her
most fiery, orange kisses.
At night, the entire stars tickle me with their tender,
sweet winks.
Surrounded with love like this,
How is it divinely possible to be lonely?

145

Love awakens

We are the micro-cosmic life-form of the universe.
Our very essence is not different from that of the sky
or the earth or the ants.
All is woven together by a song that is unsung yet.
Like wings, we open and close, we stumble and fall down
and then we rise
That is not all we are. We are the field where falling and
rising occurs, where dream and awakening arise.
The way we open our entire self
and pour light into the world
the way we receive love
and transmit a golden light;
makes all wings expand and touch each other in gratitude.
The mountain bows to the valley, the forest drinks
light from the sun
In this touching love awakens in all beings.

Blessed Is the One

Affluence
is what we already are.
deficiency is what the ego creates.
until the seashells know the sea as themselves
they will keep chiming and clinking.
Blessed is the one who's married to
the source from where all things emanate.
and to where all things return.

Someone Has Opened This Chest

Someone
has opened this chest and infused it
with immense innocence.
and even in the middle of great crisis
all that is felt is deep gratitude.
We see beauty like this,
catch flame then melt forever.
The truth is
We are not here to explain theories
We are here to experience love.

Who Are You?

We're rising beyond the seasons
of waiting, my friend
because your eyes want to see something more stunning.
The one who truly loves you is here already
to take away your future
and steal your past from you.
Then who are you, my friend
after all your content is totally gone
after your fear of being secure evaporates;
Who are you that remains undamaged
and untouched?

Ever Since I Heard About You

Ever since I heard about you,
I've been taking down
curtains after curtains after curtains
until I was able to see your face.
Now I know with all my heart,
why everyone who sits here, with you,
tastes like a sweet wine.

The Thousand Dormant Volcanoes

Here is what happens
most elegant one:
Every moment I remember you
Countless stars in this body,
The thousand dormant volcanoes,
The music I have never heard before,
the flowers no one ever smelled
Come alive again.

The Sea Swims Through You

My dear one:
I don't want you
To come to me as a casualty.
The moon might be eclipsed, might wane
Or covered by a cloud.
Have you ever seen her running out of her smiles?
Now, leave all your woes behind and listen:
The sea is swimming through you.

The Hands

When you know
You are the sun
blazing the entire sky,
The hands
that build walls around you
will quickly start shaking.

Lion's Roar

Sometimes
We feel the depth and intensity
Of beauty around us
And dissolve into tears.
And in every drops of tears
You can hear the lion's roar
And the ocean singing
Of union.

When We're Ready to Drink

My daughter and I went for a walk
stepping on piles of fallen leaves.
The trees stood naked and yet firm and awake
bowing and whirling to every sunlight traveling.
The path in the woods gives off delicious breath
touching and healing every feet she comes in touch with.
Flowers, my friend, flowers
drop their soft petals
to a roaring wind
and still their fragrance
catches us like fire
and we fall down in prayers.
Nothing outside of you matters, my friend
As nothing inside of you matters.
Just remember to surrender all reasons, all forms.
water turns to sweet laughter only to find us again
in our glass when we are ready to drink.

Like a Tree

You struggle, you toil my dear friend,
to survive.
Like a tree in the rainforest, plant yourself
firmly, deeply into your heart
and then dance gracefully
with every breeze that comes
your way.

Saving the World

I know, dear one
You've always wanted to save the world from falling
apart,
To end the wars in the Middle East, to feed the hungry
And to take down the authoritarian
regimes in Africa and elsewhere.
But dear one
with your own anger in side of you,
With your own fear inside of you
With your own wanting inside of you
With your own wars in side of you,
How can you possibly grow wings
and soar?

Drink This Light

This is enormous;
The radiance surging inside
Every little openings.
The water has fully soaked the soil
Pouring through and through.
The parts that claim to be separate
No more exist now.
Touching every particle
with one divine song.
Everything blending
into everything else.
Don't go far, my friend.
Drink this light in front of you.

The Broom

Grace is not what you love.
It is what you are.
You turn away from her
and in the blink of the eye
you meet the twins named anger and fear.
Say the words a thousand times "who am I"
"who am I" with a large space between them.
This is a broom with divine eloquence sweeping your house
From dirt.

Language of the Roses

The way rocks roll down the hill
the way feet take turn to rise and fall
the way light moves though the caves,
the way children see each other and feel the
eyes magnet
the way you get inside of me and
turn me into a jewel;
This is no imagination or wishful thinking.
It is intoxication.
It is the language of the roses.

Happiness

Living in a mansion
Or driving a luxury car
Or being a movie star
Cannot grant you happiness.
Happiness
Is how you are deeply in touch with life.
Happiness
Is how passionately and tenderly
You make love to existence
Knowing that
you are not separate from her.

Let it go

An icicle hanging down a roof
offers himself fully to the sun.
Your commutes between the ocean of fragrance
and this world is a sacred dance
You perform every day without rehearsals.
If there is anything at all
in your life
that can be taken away
from you,
let it go now.

Enter This Moment with Me

People ask
How old are you?
You pause here and reflect
because what you are going to say
could alter the chemical
 reaction of the galaxies
This is like saying
How old is life?
or when has the universe began?
or since when has a bird start singing?
Inside a single string
the cosmos pulsate with exuberance.

Barbed Wires

It rained heavily last night
taking down barbed wires and posts
standing between houses—
Only when you follow the light
in your heart, dear one,
can you break demarcations
and shine brightly.

This Being in LOVE

This being in LOVE
Weaves elegant wings around you,
lifts you up and places
you in the center of all beings and
then birth and death, lying and truth,
grief and sorrow
Are no longer your concerns.
This being in LOVE, my friend,
makes you a sweet hose
through which
innocence pours constantly.

With You

With you
I can sit in deep silence
For eternity with no desire to speak.
With you
I can soar a thousand skies
With no fear of falling down.
With you
I can lie down on a grass
With no garments on.
Oh sweet mouthed one!
Who can tell the depth of this faith
I have in you!

Your Hand Gives Off Light

Your hand,
Like a bonfire
Gives off light
And anyone you touch
Turns into a brilliant morning.
Oh! what a friend you are, dear one!
what a fire you are!
That keeps burning even
In the wildest storm.

Cracks of our lips

Some weave basket out of light
some weave love.
some gather dry woods and build fires in the hills
and then toast fresh corn and share it with the
evening breeze.
some build fire in the hearts and let it spread
until it consumes the entire world.
Look my friend:
from the outside, it seems we do things differently.
from inside
the stillness of a poem can hold the ocean.
we recite every word with the heart full of song,
the ocean pours into the cracks of our lips.

Inside a Goat

Don't be fooled
by appearance
dear friend—
A tiger roars
from inside a goat.
The sky moves
through a falcon's feathers—
don't be afraid to break
into dust—
grapes nourish our
souls only when they
are crushed and squeezed—
after all
nothing is in
your control.
Only remembering
can expand you.
Not from memory
but from intelligence—
You've a center
that is unshakably sweet—
that has infinite evergy
to weave turmoil
into wine.

The Gathering of Moons

We meet the gathering of moons in the heart of the sky
and would say, "these are brilliant human beings."
Then after a short while we run into human beings
shining like milky ways and whisper
"what radiant suns are these!"
Then again we meet all beings
underneath a tiny raindrop and say
is there any difference between making love
to the beloved and losing oneself to innocence?

The wall between us

This morning
on my way to work,
my eyes were fixed on the wild sky
vanishing into the sun's beautiful body.
This is how we all disappear
into each other when the walls between
us come down.

The Bus

I went by bus today
From my suburban home to downtown Minneapolis
And then to work.
How I loved watching life happening in the bus!
Even though it is still autumn,
Winter's song is already here and everyone
was dressed in warm clothes.
I watched the sea of people leaving the bus at every stop
And new wave of people coming aboard.
The bus said nothing to those who left
And to the ones who came in.
She is never married to anyone nor divorced from anyone.
For those who wanted to leave, she kept her doors wide open
For the ones who wanted to come in, her seats were
warm and welcoming.
Friends cross our path, stumble on our footprints, pause
a little bit and then enter our heart and mind or we enter theirs.
After a while either they part or we leave.
Story ends there but life continues. Pain of separation continues.
Suffering continues until we learn a true freedom like the bus,
the art of letting go, the wisdom of non-attachment.